MW01065092

"YOU'RE THE REASON OUR KIDS ARE UGLY"

"YOU'RE THE REASON OUR KIDS ARE UGLY"

and Other Gems of Country Music Wisdom

★

Merrit Malloy & Emerald Rose

HarperPerennial

A Division of HarperCollins*Publishers*

FIRST EDITION

ISBN 0-06-273363-X (pbk)
95 96 97 98 99 ❖/HC 10 9 8 7 6 5 4 3 2 1

Contents

Preface

After years of collecting quotes, I've found none more quotable than the genuinely funny, refreshingly honest and deeply philosophic words from the world of Country. It is (after all) the language of the real people. "We're just folks," my friend Buck says, "... we don't try to save the world; we have enough trouble trying to get our lawn mowers started." I'm still not sure if they're putting us all on or if these easygoing, exceptionally friendly folks are just born with the ability to say exactly what they mean in such a way that it actually means what it says.

"Don't Squat With Yer Spurs On!" Texas Bix Bender writes—and that's about as good advice as you can get.

Sure, a lot of it is tongue in cheek, and sure, Country is the soap opera of language—full of joy, celebration, heartbreak, pain, and a good bit of whining. But it's terribly true and real, like life. And so, Country has become, over years of its being so true, a language in and of itself. Not just a separate dialect but actually another way of saying things. Country is saying the same things we all say, but it speaks more clearly. Country has come up out of the King's English to become the true Words of the People.

"You can't get ahead of anybody you're tryin' to get even with," Gladiola Montana says. She goes on—listen up, diplomatic corps—"There are two kinds of people in this world: those who believe there are two kinds of people, and those who know better."

Nobody's wiser than somebody who's not trying to be wise. And nobody has more fun than the folks who just live instead of trying to live as if they're somebody. Country folk know that we're all pretty much the same—that we all want love, a good home, food on the table, a few laughs, some good friends. They know that we're all much more alike than we are different. It's this awareness of being human that marks their words.

Nobody has more to say more often than the folks. And frankly, nobody says it better.

We hope that you'll treasure this volume, not only as a delicious collection of funny, ironic, uniquely Country words, but also as a book of unrepeatable wisdom.

As Buck's Grandmother, Letty, sums it up, "Have a day."

Eat your heart out, Socrates! Here come the folks in the big white hats. The Country folks. America's (and life's) true voices.

Merrit Malloy

DOWN HOME

You got to have smelt a lot of mule manure
before you can sing like a hillbilly.

Hank Williams

I was born so far back in a Kentucky hollow that
you had to break daylight with a sledgeham-
mer, and the groundhogs carried the mail.

Molly O'Day (1923–1987)

You guys are as unlucky as a one-legged man
at an ass kickin'. . .

Jethro's dad [of Homer and Jethro]

"Yonder Comes a Sucker"

Jim Reeves

Hal fell through his asshole and hung himself.

DJ Hal Harris' reaction to meeting Patsy Cline,
as told by super-fan Louise Seger

David Allan Coe, he ain't worth a fart to me. His music ain't no good. . . I guess there's some people that'd want to hit me in the head about it. Maybe David Allan Coe.

Country Music Fan Shannon Lee

★ 4 ★

I'd call her [Loretta Lynn] and she'd say, "I can't record. I'm canning sausage."

Producer Omar Bradley

We used to say that the rest of us kids were homemade, but Ricky was store-bought.

Ricky Van Shelton's sister revealing that
Ricky was the only one born in a hospital

"(Old Dogs, Children and) Watermelon Wine"

Tom T. Hall

Roy [Clark] put the Haw in Hee Haw.

Eleanor Schwartz, *Life* magazine

"T-Bone Talkin' Woman With a Hot Dog Heart"

Billy Edd Wheeler

[We fought] like two cats with their tails tied together thrown over a clothesline.

Wynona and Naomi Judd

. . . She's as country as a can o' kraut.

Jeanne Pruett about Emmylou Harris

If you don't like the Marshalls' music, you've got stone ears and a lead heart.

Bluegrass Unlimited about Ohio's gospel-singing

Mrs. Tugwell just had her sixteenth young 'un. She said she had so many young 'uns, she'd run out of names—to call her husband!

Minnie Pearl

I'm basically a country gal, a country song-writer, and a country singer. I could probably sing "Stardust," but it ain't nearly as pretty to me as "Wild Side of Life."

Jeanne Pruett

COUNTRY
WISDOM

"Don't Come Home a Drinkin' with Lovin' on Your Mind"

Loretta Lynn

Just keep your chin up and your skirt down.

Del Wood and Patsy Cline's advice
to women in country music

"Mammas, Don't Let Your Babies
Grow Up to Be Cowboys"

Waylon Jennings and Willie Nelson

Just love them, honey, and they'll
love you right back.

Judge Hay to Grand Ole Opry's
nervous newcomer Minnie Pearl

Keep your boots on, keep your jeans on, and keep it country.

Arista Records' advice to Ronnie Dunn and Kix Brooks

Right now, there's two things you don't need: a wife and a dog, 'cause you ain't home enough to take care of either one of 'em.

Dad's advice to Kenny Chesney

All right ladies, you don't want to ignore the captain. Fasten your sanitary belts!

Patsy Cline

"Don't Give Candy to a Stranger"

Larry Boone

Hoss, if you can't do it with feeling, *don't*.

Patsy Cline to Dottie West

ON STAGE AND ON THE ROAD

. . . There wasn't a whole lot of difference between dealing with a room full of kindergartners and a barroom full of drunks.

Nanci Griffith, a former teacher

An Opry audience can be as cold as a January night in Nome if a non-Opry member does an act they don't like.

Minnie Pearl

People don't come to the shows to see you be you. They come to see you be *them* and what they want to be. I've always believed that.

Dolly Parton

Some acts feel like the world owes them a living. But me, I owe them, and when a fan buys a ticket to my show, he owns me for two hours. I've got a million bosses.

Faron Young

I was invited to Nashville to perform on
The Grand Ole Opry. For a month I was briefed,
as though I were going to a foreign country and
should know all the rules of protocol. I was told
I was going to meet Little Jimmy Dickens,
Roy Acuff, Red Foley, Minnie Pearl,
Hank Williams, and Ernest Tubb. I kept saying,
"yes, yes," and trying to remember their names.
To me, it was like trying to remember the
names of Lithuanian royalty.

Margaret Whiting, the first woman to have a No. 1 hit
on the newly established country chart

There's something that happens on stage when the crowd's with you and the lights are just right and the sound is good. There's a magic that just seems to unfold and, until someone has experienced it themselves, you can't explain it. It's like telling someone what oysters taste like.

T.G. Sheppard

The old circuits sometimes called for five shows a day. I learned to sleep in the car, get ready in five minutes, and tune a guitar in two. Sometimes I felt like I had little wool sweaters on my teeth. My body ached. Then I stopped a show with a routine, and I finally had to face it—I was hooked.

June Carter

The first time I ever sang in a bar, I almost cried. I was used to having all the attention focused on us. In church everyone was quiet and listened. This was, get 'em a drink, go to the bathroom, smoke a cigarette, talkin'. It was a real culture shock.

Kim Forester

We were all swallowing enough pills to choke Johnny Cash when he was at his worst.

Willie Nelson

When they called 'em rock and roll pioneers, they were talking about the music. But that pretty much described the living conditions too.

Waylon Jennings on his days touring with Buddy Holly

Before I ever came to the Opry, I had a better dressing room than this. And it was a crapper, too.

Patsy Cline

After every tour, I swear it'll be my last. But after I'm home for a couple days, I'm ready to go back on the road.

Willie Nelson

My music is Saturday-night-in-a-pickup-truck-with-the-windows-rolled-down-having-a-good-time-party music.

David Lee Murphy

I don't know why anyone would want to hear me. I sound like a damned frog.

Kris Kristofferson

We used to have a saying at the Opry. "Nobody likes us but the people."

Minnie Pearl

Kick off your shoes, let 'em roll down the aisle.
We'll sort 'em out later. You might even get a
better pair.

Sunshine Sue (1912–1979),
to audiences of the "Old Dominion Barn Dance,"
heard on CBS radio

COUNTRY
HUMOR

They say that Virginia is the mother of Texas.
We never knew who the father was, but we
kinda suspected Tennessee.

Tex Ritter

"Your Name May Be Chardonnay (But There's
Moonshine in Your Eyes)"

Roy Blount, Jr. [Song title suggested in a dream]

One reason I'm here t-t-tonight is to d-d-dispel those r-r-rumors going around that M-M-Mel T-T-Tillis has quit st-st-stuttering. That's not t-t-true. I'm still st-st-stuttering—and I'm m-m-making a pretty good l-l-living at it t-t-too.

Mel Tillis

"Let's Be Together Forever Till Boggy Gets Out on Parole"

Roy Blount, Jr. [Song title suggested in a dream]

We play mandolin and guitar. We play by ear. It's very awkward but it saves wear and tear on our fingers.

Homer and Jethro

The doctors and nurses were all so good to me. As I was leaving, I asked, "Oh, how in the world will I ever be able to repay you all?" And they told me, "By check, money order, or cash."

Donna Fargo on her ongoing battle with multiple sclerosis

. . . How would you like to try turning "You Can't Have Your Kate and Edith Too" into Farsi, or "I'm Gonna Rent a U-Haul and Haul You All Away" into Japanese?

Roy Blount, Jr.

Hell, I've been everywhere and done everything—twice. I've been up and down like a windowshade.

Johnny Paycheck

You know how to find Texas? You just go east till you smell it and south till you step in it! And you always know when you cross the Texas line 'cause your wife starts bitchin' and your kids wanta piss and you feel like goin' and stealin' somethin'.

Waylon Jennings

"I'm Gonna Hire a Wino to Decorate Our Home"

David Frizzell

. . . At one time I was singing about eight hours a day, and a doctor checked my throat for a cold and said, "Jesse, you don't have any vocal cords. You've got vocal *cables*."

Jesse Hunter

Do you know who the greatest act in the world is? It's whoever closed the night before we open in a club.

Homer and Jethro

Pam Tillis sang, "Call Me Cleopatra, I'm the Queen of Denial." But we're following that with "You Wouldn't Call Me Passive-Aggressive If You Knew How Much It Hurts."

Roy Blount, Jr.

Their name suggests a band of wild pygmies stalking the hills of Appalachia, the local folk afraid to go out at night lest a blowgun find its target, and their shrunken heads fated to hang from the rear-view mirror of a two-toned Chevy.

From a Mercury/Polygram press
release about The Kentucky Headhunters

All the women then tried to have hourglass figures, and a lot of them looked as if the sand had all run into the bottom of the glass!

The Duke of Paducah

Our voices are trained but not housebroken.

Homer and Jethro

I've been broke before and will be again. . . I been callin' around, lookin' for one of them suicide machines. I'll go on national TV, hook myself up to that machine, and tell everyone I have till seven o'clock to get 16 million. If I don't get it, I'm pulling the plug.

Willie Nelson

I guess I'd give just about anything I own to have written the Bellamy Brothers' "If I Said You Had a Beautiful Body (Would You Hold It Against Me?)." Not the song, just the title. I have, in fact come up with the following title, which may be deemed more appropriate to these times of political sensitivity:
"If I Said 'If I Said You Had a Beautiful Body (Would You Hold It Against Me?)' Would You Hold It Against Me?"

Roy Blount, Jr.

We have decided to tell all, fully realizing that our threat to Hemingway could easily end up as wall-to-wall carpeting on the bottom of bird cages all over the world.

The beginning of a never-published
autobiography of Homer and Jethro

MARRIAGE. . . AND DIVORCE

I made a good match when I married and settled down. My wife was really prominent—in Washington, Chicago, New York—and around the hips.

The Duke of Paducah

Gerald [Cline] sealed the bonds of matrimony several times and, I think, each time with invisible glue.

Nevin Cline, Patsy Cline's brother-in-law

The thrice-divorced Carlene [Carter] calls her
pickers The Better-Than-a-Husband-Band,
"because they don't give me no shit."

Finding Her Voice: The Saga of Women In Country Music

"She Got the Gold Mine (I Got the Shaft)"

Jerry Reed

I'm divorced and I've been to the circus and I've seen the clowns. This ain't my first rodeo.

Naomi Judd

If love is blind, marriage is an eye-opener.

Lois Troxell discussing her friend
Patsy Cline's first marriage

You get married then [at age 15] either because you're stupid or you're pregnant. Unfortunately, I was both.

Carlene Carter

"All My Ex's Live in Texas"

George Strait

We all make mistakes. I got married when I was
seventeen. You can't top that one.

Naomi Judd

I don't believe in alimony—it's too much like
buying hay for a dead horse.

The Duke of Paducah

"Sleeping Single in a Double Bed"

Barbara Mandrell

No. Every two years I'm just going to buy a woman that I don't like a new house.

Travis Tritt's response to whether
he is ready to remarry

"Remember the Alamo-ny"

Song Title by Barbara Fairchild

My wife told me that if I left her, I'd be throwing away my life, whereupon I replied, "Well, it's my life—I guess I can throw it away if I want to." As soon as I said the line, my songwriter's antenna went up, and it didn't take me long to write the song. I thought it turned out to be pretty clever, but the humor and poignancy were totally lost on my wife's divorce lawyer.

Bill Anderson

One night I came home drunk and passed out. This was my first marriage, the early days in Nashville, and we were living in a trailer. Anyway, I came home drunk as usual and went to sleep, and my wife was really pissed. So she took a needle and thread and calmly wrapped a sheet around me and sewed me up in the sheet. She took a broom and started beating the crap out of me. . . It's good that this was before they started cuttin' things off.

Willie Nelson

"You're the Reason Our Kids Are Ugly"

Loretta Lynn and Conway Twitty

When we took time out to have children,
we tried to have them close to each other
so the kids could be with each other while
we're working. It kind of irks our husbands
a little because we consult each other
before we consult with them.

Sisters Kristine Oliver Arnold and Janis Oliver,
Sweethearts of The Rodeo

The night of our honeymoon my husband took one look and said, "Is that all for me?"

Dolly Parton

You know, for years my husband wouldn't let me wear makeup or cut my hair. To shave my legs, I had the children watch at the doors and windows in case he came home.

Loretta Lynn

Single mother, thy name is Guilt.

Pam Tillis

COUNTRY PHILOSOPHY

Grin when you bare it—it's the only way.

Dolly Parton

"Too Dumb for New York City, Too Ugly for L.A."
[Album title]

Waylon Jennings

I'm a Frisbeetarian. We worship frisbees®. We believe when you die your soul goes up on the roof and you can't get it down.

Jim Stafford

My philosophy has always been to shoot
straight, make sure you're the one still standing, then take your loved one's hand and move
it on. More than that, no one can ask for. And
more than that, no one really needs.

Willie Nelson

"I Don't Mind the Thorns (If You're the Rose)"

Lee Greenwood

There was a black preacher I heard one time who said, "The best thing you can do for the poor is not to be one of them."

Merle Haggard

Every day oughta be Christmas and every night should be New Year's Eve.

Bobby Bare

"You're the Reason God Made Oklahoma"

David Frizzell and Shelly West

There's a little country in all of us,
a little frontier.

Louis L'Amour

They say a mind is a terrible thing to waste.
Well, I say a dream is a terrible thing to waste.

Dolly Parton

There are good ol' boys in the Bronx.

Aaron Tippin

After all, even a bad night of music beats the best day you'll ever have in the heating and air-conditioning business.

Travis Tritt

This ole gal used to think happiness resulted when my earnings matched my yearnings.

Patsy Cline

Someone told me that both guitars and horses will take you for a ride, but horses buck harder.

Jesse Hunter

I'm gonna give it a while. If it stinks, I'll never do it again. If it's great, I'll say I knew all along.

Toby Keith about acting in a movie

The way I see it, if you want the rainbow, you gotta put up with the rain.

Dolly Parton

Success is having to worry about every damned thing in the world except money.

Johnny Cash

When people say less is more, I say more is more. Less is less. I go for more.

Dolly Parton

My wife said to me: "You're always trying to get something for nothing! Don't you realize that hard work never hurt anybody?" I said, "Yeah, I realize that, and I don't want to take any chances on spoiling its record!"

The Duke of Paducah

IN THE BEGINNING. . .

I thought: "Oh, my God: I'm going to die, and the only thing I'll be remembered for is a hemorrhoid commercial. Girl, you have got to give this singin' thing one more try."

K.T. Oslin

 Several people woke up.

Minnie Pearl's mother when asked how she thought the audience responded to her daugher's Grand Ole Opry debut.

I called him three times and was turned down. Finally, I just sat on his steps one morning and waited with my guitar beside me. He came up and evidently he'd had a good night. So I said: "I'm Johnny Cash. I think if you'd listen to me that you'd be glad you did." That line has never failed me. He said: "Well, come on in. Let's hear it."

Johnny Cash on how he met Sam Phillips,
credited with discovering him.

Papa was going to Los Angeles on a business
trip and asked Mama and me if we wanted to
go. Does a sinner want to go to heaven?
L.A. meant music to me. Mama worried about
clothes while I worried about getting
all my songs in one briefcase. . . Papa said
I was squirrelly.

Cindy Walker on how she came
to L.A. and songwriting fame

Kris [Kristofferson] was a janitor at CBS. He used to slip tapes of his songs into my wife's purse. The next time he saw me, he'd say, "Did you hear that song?" I'd say, "Not yet, but I will." And this went on for a long time. . . Then one Sunday afternoon he landed a helicopter out here in my yard. . . fell out with a beer in one hand and a tape in the other, and said, "You're gonna listen to my song." I said, "Come on in." I listened to "Sunday Morning Coming Down." I listened to all his songs after that.

Johnny Cash

. . . In the daytime I got a map of the stars' homes and went around and left my album off at everybody's house. Like that was gonna get me a record deal, you know?

Suzy Bogguss on her early Nashville days

We'd live in one place for a month, then pick up and move when the rent would come due. We didn't have any money, but I did have some new songs I thought I could sell to somebody.

Willie Nelson

I always loved music, but I was so shy that when my mother would ask me to sing for company, I'd go out into the kitchen and sing "How Far is Heaven" real loud so they could hear me, but I wouldn't have to look at them.

Patty Loveless

I didn't like picking cotton one bit. . . I used to stand in the fields and watch the cars go by and think, "I want to go with them."

Willie Nelson

MEN AND
WOMEN

I don't know how a man's mind works. If I did,
I'd be a millionaire—I'd sell a tip sheet.

K.T. Oslin

"I Want My Rib Back"

Keith Whitley

I don't know whether the girls I went out with
had willpower or not—but they sure did have
won't power!

The Duke of Paducah

The men have enough going for 'em in this life. We women have got to stick together.

Loretta Lynn

"A Headache Tomorrow (Or a Heartache Tonight)"

Mickey Gilley

"John's Been Shucking My Corn"

Onie Wheeler

"I'm Gonna Sleep With One Eye Open"

Flatt and Scruggs

I'm not telling anybody, "If you're not happy, go out and screw around, because your wife will become a dynamo for you," but I got to be honest with you, that's what happened for me.

Garth Brooks

"I Cheated Me Right Out of You"

Moe Bandy

★ 67 ★

"You Two-Timed Me One Time Too Often"

Tex Ritter

"Don't Cheat in Our Hometown"

Ricky Skaggs

I woke up on the right side of the wrong bed
this morning.

Jeannie Seely

"Let's Fall to Pieces Together"

George Strait

You're always talking about your career but all I hear are hims, hims, hims, and this ain't church.

Fay Crutchley to Patsy Cline

"Our Love is on the Faultline"

Crystal Gayle

"Get Your Biscuits in the Oven and Your
Buns in Bed"

Kinky Friedman

"If I Said You Had a Beautiful Body (Would You
Hold it Against Me?)"

The Bellamy Brothers

"You're Gonna Ruin My Bad Reputation"

Ronnie McDowell

Women are the best things in the world to write about. They got it all—so what better subject than women. . . oh, and whiskey?

Dean Dillon

COUNTRY LEGENDS

[Patsy Cline was]. . . the first woman who could make me feel like crying out of one eye and winking out of the other!

Anonymous

"You're the meanest bitch I ever met."

Producer Owen Bradley to Patsy Cline during a frustrating recording session

Hank [Williams] had an awfully big ego. Tried to write a song every time he picked up a guitar. . . he'd come up real close to you and say, "Listen to this, hoss," and he'd sing "Jambalaya" or "Hey, Good Lookin,'" and that bourbon breath would knock you down and he'd say, "How you like that?" "Great, Hank." He'd say, "You damn right it is."

Chet Atkins

Dolly [Parton] knew exactly what she wanted to be. She sat right on my couch one day and said, "When you son-of-a-bitches learn how to sell a female Elton John with long hair and big boobs that dresses like a freak, then we'll make some money."

Jerry Bradley, then head of RCA's country division

He was singing and split his pants. One of his boys went to get him another pair and threw the split pair in the corner. A girl who was working for the Methodist Publishing Company in the same building asked me what to do with the pants and I told her, "You better hang onto them, that boy's gonna be famous." She said, "Naw," and there she was six months later on "I've Got a Secret" with Elvis's pants.

Chet Atkins

With her amazing hair and her amazing, um, figure, Dolly [Parton] never had trouble getting noticed. Problem was, the men who ran Nashville always noticed that stuff more than they noticed her talent—which was even bigger than, um, well, you know.

Eleanor Schwartz, *Life* magazine

All I wanted to be was *Hank* Williams, and suddenly I was Andy.

Roger Miller

I ain't no star. A star is something up in the night sky. People say to me, "You're a legend." I'm not a legend. I'm just a woman.

Loretta Lynn

Well, you're a conceited little son-of-a-bitch!. . . You don't say hello, kiss my ass, or nothin' else!

Patsy Cline

[Patsy Cline] taught me a lot about show
business, like how to go on a stage and
how to get off.

Loretta Lynn

For a long time I thought Mother and Aunt Sara
and Uncle A.P. turned into tiny people who
fit inside the radio or behind our little
crank-up Victrola.

Anita Carter about her legendary family The Carters

I wouldn't say Patsy [Cline] was rated X, but she'd come in under R!

Brenda Lee

It ain't what you got, it's what you put out; and, boys, I can deliver.

Uncle Dave Macon

My voice ain't what I call pleasin'. My heart is always true, but the notes that come out ain't.

Dolly Parton

You wouldn't have to tell Patsy [Cline] anything about this women's lib business. I do believe she could have taught them a thing or two.

Owen Bradley

Bill [Monroe] didn't know how Elvis would do on 'Blue Moon of Kentucky,' but when the Brinks truck pulled up with 'mail,' he sent Elvis his whole catalogue!

Ricky Skaggs

To hell with President Roosevelt, to hell with Babe Ruth, and to hell with Roy Acuff.

Insult used by Japanese pilots to heckle Americans in WWII—as reported by Ernie Pyle

Patsy [Cline] had magnetism but she also had a pair of balls. Her heart was bigger than she was.

Faron Young

I'm sure, physically, I could have knocked the hell out of Patsy Cline. But if I'd have hit her a couple of times, she'd of picked up a damned chair or something and let me have it. You know, you're not gonna run over Patsy. Not me or anybody else.

Husband Charlie Dick

HARD TIMES

"Things Aren't Funny Anymore"

Merle Haggard

There was a period of time there that I seriously considered taking up hard drinking as an occupation.

Joe Ely

"Who'll Buy My Memories: The IRS Tapes"

The name of the album Willie Nelson recorded to pay off part of his $32 million debt to the IRS

"The Whisky Ain't Workin"

Travis Tritt and Marty Stuart

I live my songs too strongly.

George Jones

"Over the Hills to the Poorhouse"

Flatt and Scruggs

"You Could've Heard a Heart Break"

Johnny Lee

If you really want to try something unusual, try passing out in front of five thousand people.

Loretta Lynn

"Who's Gonna Mow Your Grass"

Buck Owens

I was in a phase at that time when I was eating a lot of Cap'n Crunch. . .

Eddie Rabbit

"Love Don't Care (Whose Heart it Breaks)"

Earl Thomas Conley

"I Guess it Never Hurts to Hurt Sometimes"

The Oak Ridge Boys

Most of the stories behind most of my songs
are simply hunger.

Songwriter Ben Peters

HEY, GOOD LOOKIN'...

The video thing has put too much emphasis on appearance. I'll tell you, if me and Willie [Nelson] were starting out now, we'd be in a lot of trouble.

Waylon Jennings

"Do You Love as Good as You Look"

The Bellamy Brothers

What we're going to have to do to be popular in country music is to get into an ass-wiggling contest. . .

> Travis Tritt on the success of
> Billy Ray Cyrus and the Achy Break dance

I just don't get it. Hell, he's just an old, fat, bald cowboy.

> The concert date of an avid Garth Brooks fan

. . . It's not true about me having problems with anything to do with my breasts, other than they seem to be killing a lot of other people.

Dolly Parton

I had a crooked nose from a fight with a paratrooper in a honky-tonk, a scar on my cheek left by a drunken German doctor who couldn't find a cyst he was trying to remove, and a left ear with the hearing temporarily impaired because a German girl stuck a pencil in it. . . Other than that [I] was in good shape.

Johnny Cash

You'd be surprised how much it costs to look this cheap.

Dolly Parton

[Garth] Brooks has been described as having a face like "a thumb with a hat on it."

Forbes magazine

With me, it's the bigger the hair is, the more confidence I have.

Bobbie Cryner

Mel Tillis: Look, Dolly Parton's out in the audience.

Band Member: That's not Dolly Parton. That's two bald-headed men sitting together.

Did I ever use silicone? They ain't got that much plastic.

Dolly Parton

At eleven I looked eighteen. My mother said I came into the world with a training bra on.

Barbara Pittman

[After turning down both Playboy and Penthouse to pose nude.] I just feel that I'm too intelligent to have to take my clothes off to get somebody's attention.

Charly McClain

"I've Never Gone to Bed With an Ugly Woman (But I Sure Woke Up With a Few)"

Bobby Bare

Randy Hughes: Do you think Patsy [Cline]'s got
sex appeal?

Grandpa Jones: She's really got it. Just like the
stink off an ole hog!

I had my boobs lifted. . . It was more a reconstruction job, because I lost a lot of weight and they started to droop a bit. . . I just wanted to lift them off the street.

Dolly Parton

I'm not offended by all the dumb blonde jokes because I know I'm not dumb. And I also know that I'm not blonde.

Dolly Parton

THE COUNTRY
WAY

I heard a noise in the barn the other day. I went down there. My brother bought a new mule and he was trying to get the mule through the barn door but he couldn't get the mule through the barn door because the mule's ears was too long. So brother had a saw and he was sawing off the top of the barn door to get the mule in. I said, "It's a dirt floor, why don't you just dig a trench and take him in that way?" And brother said, "It ain't his legs that's too long, it's his ears!"

Minnie Pearl

My daddy's mother, my grandmother, was an inspiration to me. She was four foot eleven, weighed about a hundred and five pounds, and had nine kids. On her eighty-fifth birthday she went bowlin' and bowled one-sixty-eight!

Tammy Wynette

. . . When I was growing up in the mountains, "Be a good neighbor," people used to say, "but carry a big stick."

Billy Edd Wheeler

My grandmother said that when someone was tall, dark, and handsome, they were someone to be looked upon carefully, and if they were a tall, dark, handsome *stranger*, you'd get the women and the kids in. . .

Buck Owens

I remember being in Kentucky, and they kept me locked up because the judge's grandmother died, and nobody got out of jail till he got back. He went to the funeral, and, of course, he went to the wake, and it was out of town. . . I was in there for about a week.

Tom T. Hall

I think one of the reasons I'm a good boss is because you will always know what I'm a-thinkin'. I won't pout at you or treat you bad. I'll just say, "Hey, Joe, there's somethin' that's really buggin' the shit outta me. . . "

Dolly Parton

People ask us why we aren't rich after working so many years. The answer is simple. We pay our taxes.

Homer and Jethro

Hell, I don't really care if we don't catch any-thing. . . Sometimes it bothers me if they start bitin'. It interrupts me.

Bobby Bare talking about goin' fishin'

You think you're runnin' free, Jeannie, but you ain't. Like a heifer on a rope, one day you'll take off a-runnin' and almost break your neck, because that rope's tied to God's tree.

Jeannie C. Riley's mother's warning when she was running wild

There were two nice-lookin' fellers standing next to me, and one of them said to the other: "You know, I believe I recognize her. That's that Minnie Pearl. She's been down there at the Grand Ole Opry for 175 years." He said: "She carries on like she's from the country. I bet she don't know a goose from a gander." I turned around and I said: "Well, at Grinder's Switch we don't worry about that. We just put them all out there together and let 'em figure it out for themselves."

Minnie Pearl

On Saturday nights, when The Grand Ole Opry was on, we'd gather around and watch the radio.

Willie Nelson

Just havin' good ol' horse sense, you can make more money and get more done than all the people that have gotta fumble through their books to try to find an answer to somethin'.

Dolly Parton

"This Time I've Hurt Her More Than
She Loves Me"

Conway Twitty

I learned you can get killed right quick.

Roy Acuff, in response to being asked what he
learned from a serious car accident

I was the best-kept secret in country music.

Jett Williams, illegitimate daughter of Hank Williams

LIFE'S LITTLE IRONIES

Buy a suit with two pairs of pants, you burn a hole in the coat.

Hillbilly Saying

"Don't the Girls All Get Prettier at Closing Time"

Mickey Gilley

We're not "hillbillies" anymore. We're "Mountain Williams" now.

Anonymous

"Can't Even Get the Blues"

Reba McEntire

Charley Pride said to me once, "You can get away with singin' like a black. I can't."

Razzy Bailey

"Nobody in His Right Mind Would've Left Her"

George Strait

I was so bad, I made John Wayne look so good
that he won his only Oscar.

Glen Campbell about his acting
performance in "True Grit"

"Don't it Make My Brown Eyes Blue"

Crystal Gayle

"Why Have You Left the One You Left Me for?"

Crystal Gayle

Before, I was the hard-living, hard-drinking country queen. That was the image I was trying to project, and they weren't buying it. Now they're buying it, and I'm not selling.

Linda Hargrove

I've been around the world twice on one little block right here in Nashville.

Celinda Pink

"You Never Miss a Real Good Thing (Till He Says Goodbye)"

Crystal Gayle

I'm just a hippie. I think the reason I got into show business was I thought it would be the easiest way to buy a farm.

Lacy J. Dalton

. . . the most embarrassing thing that ever happened to me was when I entered a Dolly Parton look-alike contest—and lost.

Dolly Parton

THE REBEL YELL

When I was in school in the first grade, the teacher told me, she said one and one was two. I said, "Now wait a minute, how do you know?" And right then we had a big problem.

Jerry Lee Lewis

"Take this Job and Shove it"

Johnny Paycheck

You couldn't get ahead of Patsy [Cline]. If somebody farted in her direction, she'd raise her ass
and fart right back.

Faron Young

You can knock me to my knees, but you cannot
make me crawl while I'm down there.

Jeannie Seely

Those lights were hurtin' my eyes.

> Johnny Cash about his departure from
> the Grand Ole Opry in the early '60s, when he said
> goodbye by smashing all 52 stage lights

I don't know what I'd have done with me if I had
been the parent.

> Merle Haggard

There's certain people that say, "Ah, he ain't ever gonna change," but those people are just assholes, that's all. Anyone can change.

Johnny Paycheck

I've always done things differently. If Social Security picks up the tab, I just might do it again.

Jonie Mosby after giving birth at age 52 to a test-tube baby

They always used to tell me if I had a brain, I'd be dangerous. Well, I wonder if they know by now that I do. . . and I am.

Jeannie Seely

His heart's as big as his mouth.

Roger Miller about Faron Young

The first time my Mama saw me all done up with blond bleached hair all piled up and my lips, cheeks, and nails as red as I could get them, she screamed to the Lord, "Why are you testing me this way?" And she told me the Devil must have made me do it. "Heck, no," I told Mama. "Let's give credit where credit is due: I did this all myself!"

Dolly Parton

My majors in college were music and partying.
The first week on campus, I signed up for a rock
and roll group and my classes, in that order.

Pam Tillis

"I Was Country When Country Wasn't Cool"

Barbara Mandrell

When you're leaning into a curve at 60 mph and there's nothing between you and pavement but just a thin layer of leather, the last thing you're thinking about is business.

Travis Tritt

COUNTRY STYLE

I saw artists stand on their heads, gobble peanut butter from a ceiling fan, pee in a vest pocket, and all kinds of stuff, anything to be different.

Lightnin' Chance

This churnin' urn of burnin' funk could ignite fires with wet wood.

Radioman Alan Rice about Billy Ray Cyrus

Any man who can ad-lib a line on camera like, "I'm gonna get me a bottle of tequila, one of them Keno girls who can suck the chrome right off a trailer hitch, and kick back" deserves to be in movies, writing songs, or in jail.

Robert Redford about Willie Nelson in "The Electric Horseman"

With her Ivy League roots and I-can-have-it-all-stance, Mary Chapin Carpenter is to traditional country music women what Hillary Clinton is to traditional political wives.

Steve Hotchman in the *Los Angeles Times*

I prefer to go in my own direction and let someone follow me.

Roger Miller

Just when boots start looking like they're about to fall apart, that's when they're just about right.

Travis Tritt

. . . When my wife does my laundry everyone thinks an inmate lives over at our house 'cause it's just stripes up and down the line outside.

Garth Brooks

You're never sure if you want to buy her a glass of milk or a double bourbon, but a little uncertainty in life never hurt.

Ralph Novak, *People* magazine,
about Mary Chapin Carpenter

No one should wear a cowboy hat unless he feels comfortable sitting on a horse. I'm more comfortable on a Harley.

Travis Tritt

[Patsy] finally realized she could be hotter copy without a hayseed image. . . my God, she started wearing hats. Not Stetsons! Church hats, social-gathering hats. I wondered, "What next, hillbillies playing golf?"

Faron Young

My show is no-patter, no-dancing. If I scuttled all over the stage and went crazy, they'd say, "What's *that* all about?"

Roy Orbison

I don't like wimpy lyrics. I like to find things women don't normally say or are afraid to say.

Trisha Yearwood

If you have a southern accent, they automatically drop about forty IQ points from you, and if you're in a meeting with someone who's a non-southern, and you use a word that has more than three syllables in it, it takes them a while to recover.

Pat Rolfe

You don't have to have wagon wheels and hay behind you just because you're a country singer.

Charly McClain

I was always impressed with Cinderella and Mother Goose and all those things when I was a kid, because we didn't have television or movies then. I kinda patterned my look after Cinderella and Mother Goose—and the local hooker.

Dolly Parton

I just hate it [fame]. It makes me feel like I've got somethin' on the back of my skirt.

Roseanne Cash

Twang is what you feel the emotion from in country music. As "soul" is to rhythm and blues, "twang" is to country.

Janis Carnes

I've always thought that Chuck Berry might have had a rock and roll heart, but he had a country soul.

Buck Owens

[About Donny and Marie Osmond] Now they're beautiful children, and they're very talented, but they wouldn't know a country song if it hit 'em in the hind end with a broom handle!

Jean Shepard [circa 1977]

DRINKING
AND DRUGS

"She's Actin' Single (I'm Drinkin' Doubles)"

Gary Stewart

Here's to those who wish us well and those who
don't can go to hell!

A toast from Patsy Cline

"Trying to Beat the Morning Home"

T.G. Sheppard

. . . The problem is that whenever we get together he always wants to drink brandy—and after three shots of brandy, I'm always drunk. . . He talks me into it by saying things like, "It's only fruit juice, Bobby Joe."

Bobby Bare about Tom T. Hall

At 13 years of age, I figured drinking would be the meanest thing I could do.

Mac Davis

"Drinkin' My Baby (Off My Mind)"

Eddie Rabbit

I just got tired of falling down. You either
mature or you die.

Roger Miller

"Drinkin' My Baby Goodbye"

Charlie Daniels

California isn't a real good place to get
off drugs.

Waylon Jennings

If it helps to take one pill every four hours,
it must be even better to take four pills every
one hour.

Hank Williams

If you're wired, you're fired.

Willie Nelson

. . . I got to perform on TV. . . "bourbon in a glass and grass." They took the "grass" out because they thought I was talking about marijuana. I said, "No, I've got 35 head of cattle, and hay is $3.50 a bale—I LOVE grass." They didn't buy that.

Tom T. Hall

When you're bent over double and have to perform in front of thousands of people, you have
to take something to relieve it.

Tammy Wynette

LOVE AND ROMANCE

If God made anything better [than sex], he kept it for Himself.

Dottie West

"Red Neckin' Love Makin' Night"

Conway Twitty

"It Ain't Easy Bein' Easy"

Janie Frickie

Of course I want you for your body. I've got a mind of my own.

Jeannie Seely

I'm supposed to have had more men than most people change underwear.

Tanya Tucker

I want to be an 80-year-old lady whose sex life
they're still wondering about.

Dolly Parton

The robber said "Gimme your money." I said,
"But I haven't got any money," so he frisked me
and said, "Are you sure you ain't got any
money?" I said, "No sir, but if you'll do that
again I'll write you a check."

Minnie Pearl

"She Can Put Her Shoes Under My Bed (Anytime)"

Johnny Duncan

Charlie's bigger than life and twice as hard!

Patsy Cline, bragging about
her second husband

"It's Not Love (But it's Not Bad)"

Merle Haggard and the Strangers

"Let's Chase Each Other Around the Room"

Merle Haggard

I used to take long walks in the spring with pretty girls. And I used to carve our initials in the trees. Before I got married I had my initials carved in so many trees I used to get fan mail from woodpeckers.

The Duke of Paducah

It began to occur to me that there were far worse fates than working with Roy Rogers on a daily basis.

Dale Rogers

"Got the All-Overs for You"

Freddie Hart

How'd I meet her [Mrs. Brooks]? Oh, you don't wanna know this, believe me. A lot of people take this wrong. . . Sandy's very much a lady. . . I met her as a bouncer in a club and I had to throw her out of the club.

Garth Brooks

Falling in love isn't my big problem. *Staying* in love is.

Tanya Tucker

I'm having daydreams about night things in the middle of the afternoon.

John Schweers

"I've Already Loved You in My Mind"

Conway Twitty

"He's a Heartache (Looking for a Place to Happen)"

Janie Frickie

"You're So Good When You're Bad"

Charley Pride

COUNTRY
FAMILY VALUES

"I Ain't Sharin' Sharon"

Jim Stafford

I've never kissed an ass or licked a boot and I
won't ever compromise what I believe in.

Johnny Paycheck

"I Can Walk the Line (If it Ain't Too Straight)"

Joe Diffie

"Heaven's Just a Sin Away"

The Kendalls

I never sold myself out. I never went to bed with anybody unless I wanted to—never for business reasons.

Dolly Parton

I don't ever do something really weird just to get attention. It's too obvious.

Bobby Bare

"Too Much Is Not Enough"

The Bellamy Brothers with The Forester Sisters

They preached loud, spoke loud, sung
loud. . . They must have thought God
was hard of hearing!

Ricky Skaggs about his uncles

Son, I don't know you well enough to miss you when you're gone.

> Johnny Cash to his future son-in-law over the
> question of sleeping in the same bedroom
> with his fiancee, Roseanne Cash

I might have inconvenienced a few people, but I sure wasn't no Bonnie and Clyde.

> Merle Haggard

Dear God. . . I know I'm not worthy, but I need You so. Help me turn back on the right path if it's not too late. And, Lord, please let these Seventh Day Adventists get some meat in this damn hospital. I'm tired of eating all this grain!

Patsy Cline

I support our government's foreign policy.
Still. . . the only good thing that ever came from
a war is a song, and that's a hell of a way to have
to get your songs.

Johnny Cash

Sometimes I am surprised when riding along in the car, listening to a country station, at some of the subjects that are being exploited in song. I guess my generation gap is showing.

Sunshine Sue (1912–1979)

THE BUSINESS OF COUNTRY MUSIC

If I hear "demographics" one more time, I'm gonna puke right in their faces.

Johnny Cash

I'm a marketing man's nightmare. Rock and roll is really my body. My heart's country, and my soul is R&B.

Marshall Chapman

. . . you gotta understand that the music
business is basically run by Jewish people
and the image thrown up by *Kinky Friedman
and The Texas Jewboys* was not something
they wanted to promote.

David Allen Coe

If you're gonna sing a sad song, or ballad,
you've got to have lived it yourself.

George Jones

You need four things to even have a chance in this music business. To start with you need the dream, the desire to burn bright. You need the talent to back up that dream and the guts to be true to yourself about it. And you need persistence. . . But the fourth and most important thing is that you need to be blind, deaf, and dumb.

Eddie Rabbit

The best way to plug a song to me is to say, "Here's a song that you can't do, but I'd like for you to hear anyway." I'm a fool for that.

Waylon Jennings

I have no desire to be a pop artist. I couldn't go pop with a mouth full of firecrackers.

Billie Jo Spears

My producers said they were releasing it [her album] country, and I didn't even know what they were talking about.

Olivia Newton-John, who went on to win
Country Female Vocalist of the Year in 1974

I was the first of the singing cowboys. Maybe not the best, but that doesn't matter if you're first.

Gene Autrey

. . . in the late '50s, I moved back to try to make it as a writer and singer. . . Nashville was a tight clique, and my songs weren't what they considered commercial—some had more than three chords in them.

Willie Nelson

It's fate. In this business, I found out, it's 80 percent luck and 20 percent talent.

Doug Stone

Any performer who hasn't the theatrical ability to put herself into lyrics for a few minutes must have something missing—like talent.

Barbara Mandrell

I'm a seller, not a singer.

Roy Acuff

That kind of [obedient] attitude, an outasight voice and a motherfucker song—to break a chick that's all it takes. Then if she looks good and has big tits, she might just make it.

Country producer Sonny Limbo

...AND EVERYTHING IN BETWEEN

"Prop Me Up Beside the Jukebox (If I Die)"

Joe Diffie

If those ol' boys won't take me out when I'm-a livin', I sure don't want 'em taking me out when I'm dead.

Minnie Pearl on why she wants only female pallbearers

All I ever did was invent kids.

Loretta Lynn to her tablemates, scientists
and inventors at a White House dinner where
she received an Outstanding Achievement Award

He's got me listening to—what's it called?—Nine
Inch Nails? Sounds like a train wreck
sometimes, but every once in a while you
hear something good.

Waylon Jennings about his teenage son's taste in music

If you could give up fame and keep the fortune, you could go on with your life and keep going to Wal-Mart and keep spending money. And nobody would know who you are. That would be pretty darn good.

Reba McEntire

When I found myself singing over the radio, I didn't think life got much better than that.

Willie Nelson

Our life has been like Santa Claus coming to our house—and staying.

Songwriters Felice and Boudleaux Bryant

If I have any talent at all it's from God, and my mom, who was on Capitol Records also.

Garth Brooks

"Asshole from El Paso"

Kinky Friedman

"Did You Have to Bring that Up (While
I Was Eating)?"

Liz Anderson

Instead of life in prison I was doing one to fif-
teen years—I just couldn't get that to rhyme.

Merle Haggard

. . . It isn't easy. You try working "information
superhighway" into an uncomplicated title.

Roy Blount, Jr. on keeping songs current

When my time comes, just skin me and put me right up there on Trigger, just as if nothing had ever changed.

Roy Rogers

Wouldn't it be great to be a woman and be just like Willie Nelson? I've often thought, "God, would that be great, to be the first woman out there with wrinkles and not trying to cover it up."

Lacy J. Dalton